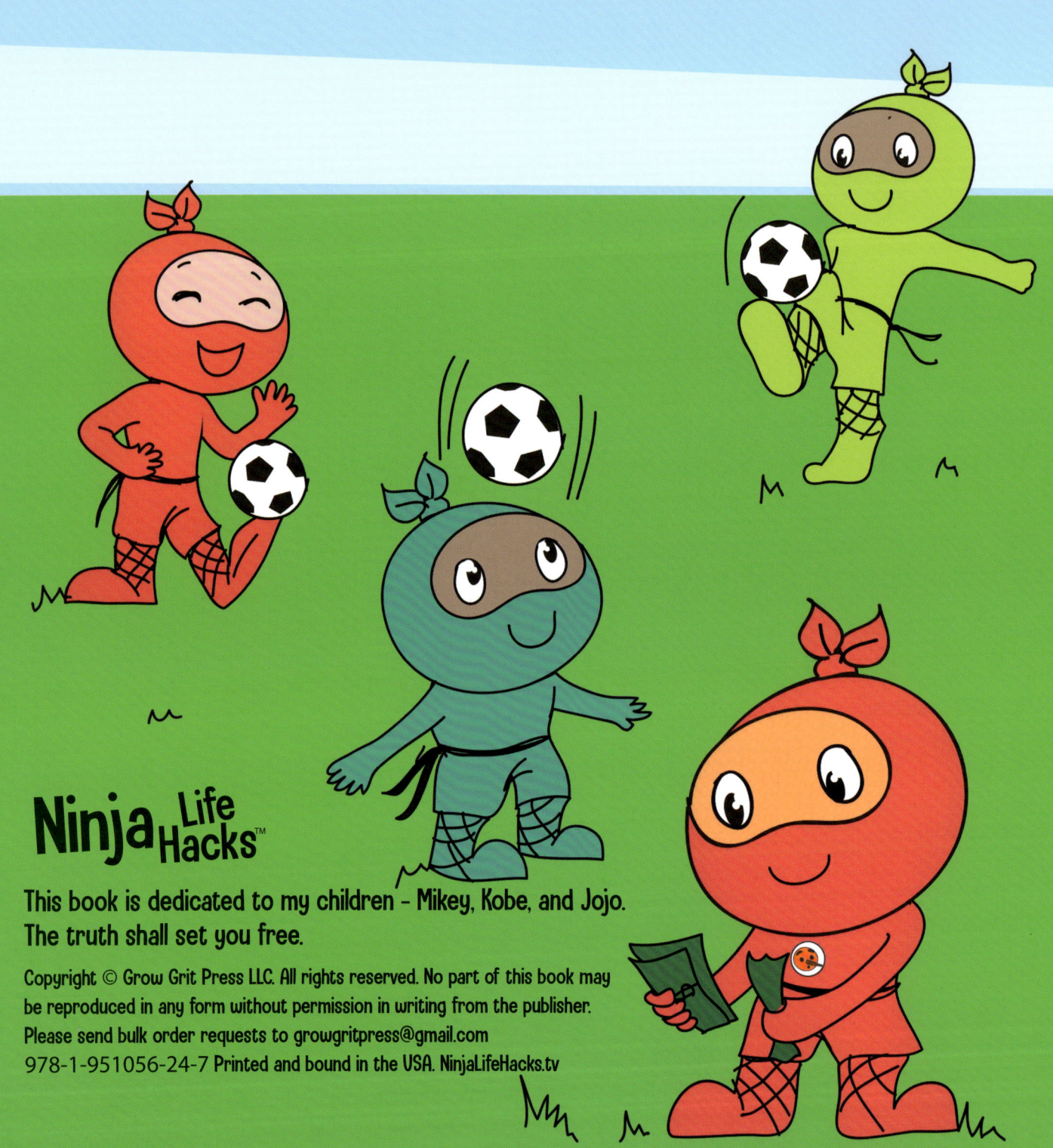

Ninja Life Hacks™

This book is dedicated to my children - Mikey, Kobe, and Jojo.
The truth shall set you free.

Copyright © Grow Grit Press LLC. All rights reserved. No part of this book may be reproduced in any form without permission in writing from the publisher.
Please send bulk order requests to growgritpress@gmail.com
978-1-951056-24-7 Printed and bound in the USA. NinjaLifeHacks.tv

Dishonest Ninja

By Mary Nhin

OFFICE

Pictures by
Jelena Stupar

I didn't think I was hurting anyone when I chose not to tell the truth.

But what I didn't understand was that each time I lied, I was hurting someone.

Because when I told a lie, it changed *me* just a little bit each time.

If I stretched the truth to impress others, it would never make me feel good enough.

When I didn't tell the truth to get something I wanted, I would worry about getting caught.

And when I lied to avoid getting into trouble, I would feel guilty for lying.

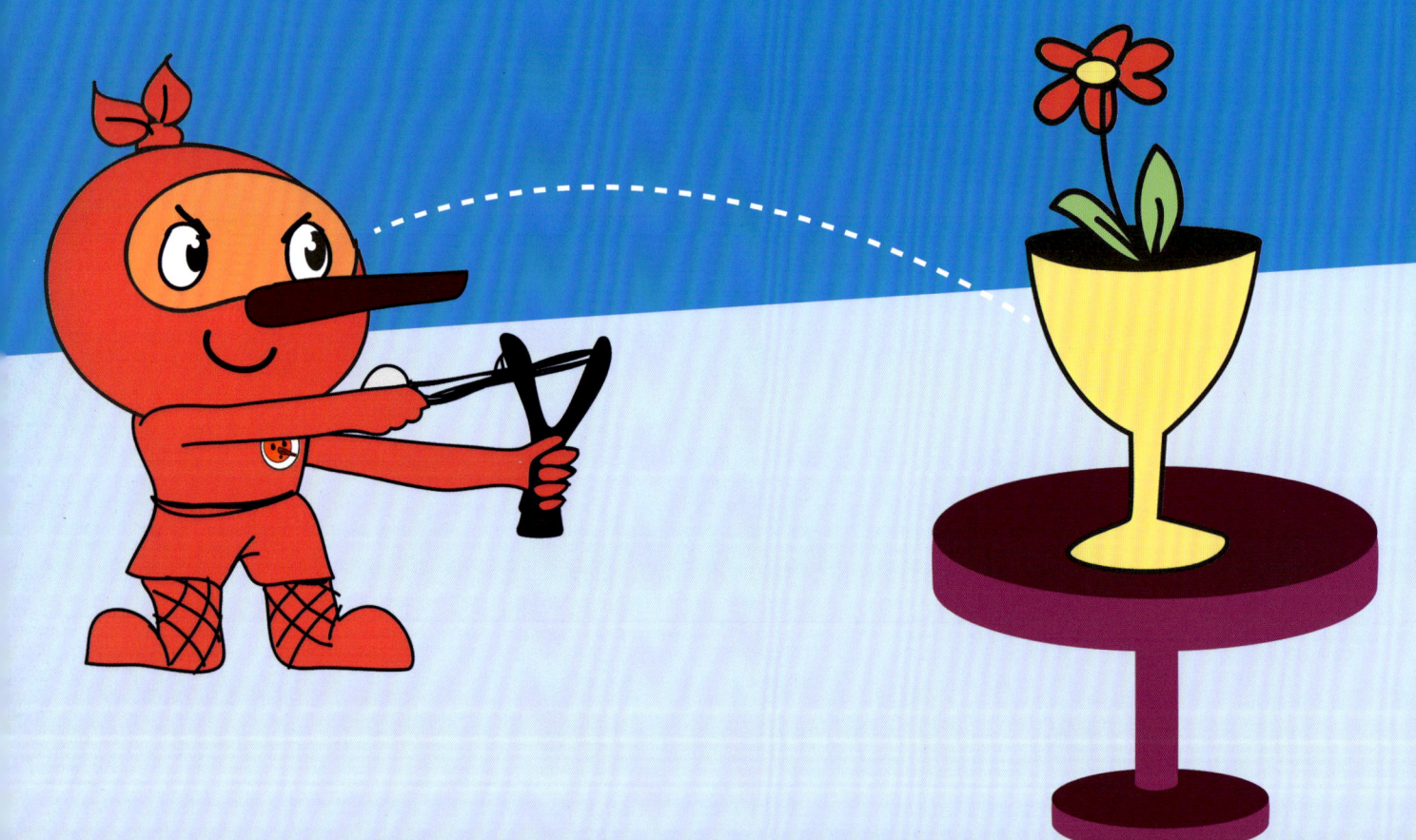

But I was forever changed after something happened one day at school...

I was playing at recess when I noticed something shiny in the grass. I picked it up and realized it was a watch.

Shy Ninja walked over and said, "Oh! That's mine."
But I insisted...

For the rest of the day, my stomach hurt. I couldn't focus. And when it came time for my favorite activity, I couldn't enjoy that either.

That evening, I could hardly eat my dinner.

From that moment on, I decided to always tell the truth, no matter what. I like the way telling the truth makes me FEEL.

Being honest helps me feel as carefree as a bird.

Your best weapon against dishonesty is to remember that telling the truth sets you free from worry and guilt.

For parent and teacher resources visit NinjaLifeHacks.tv

@marynhin @GrowGrit
#NinjaLifeHacks

Mary Nhin   Ninja Life Hacks

Ninja Life Hacks